B1 Speaking

Ten practice tests for the **Cambridge B1 Preliminary**

Anna Phillips and Terry Phillips

PROSPERITY EDUCATION

© Prosperity Education Ltd. 2025

Registered offices: Sherlock Close, Cambridge
CB3 0HP, United Kingdom

First published 2025

ISBN: 978-1-915654-48-9

Original edition © Innova Content Ltd.

This publication is in copyright. Subject to statutory exception
and to the provisions of relevant collective licensing agreements,
no reproduction of any part may take place without the written
permission of Prosperity Education.

This edition is published by arrangement with Innova Content Ltd.

The moral rights of the authors have been asserted.

'Cambridge B1 Preliminary' and 'PET' are brands belonging to The
Chancellor, Masters and Scholars of the University of Cambridge and are not
associated with Prosperity Education or its products.

Designed by ORP Cambridge

For further information and resources, visit:
www.prosperityeducation.net

To infinity and beyond.

A digital platform for Cambridge exam preparation

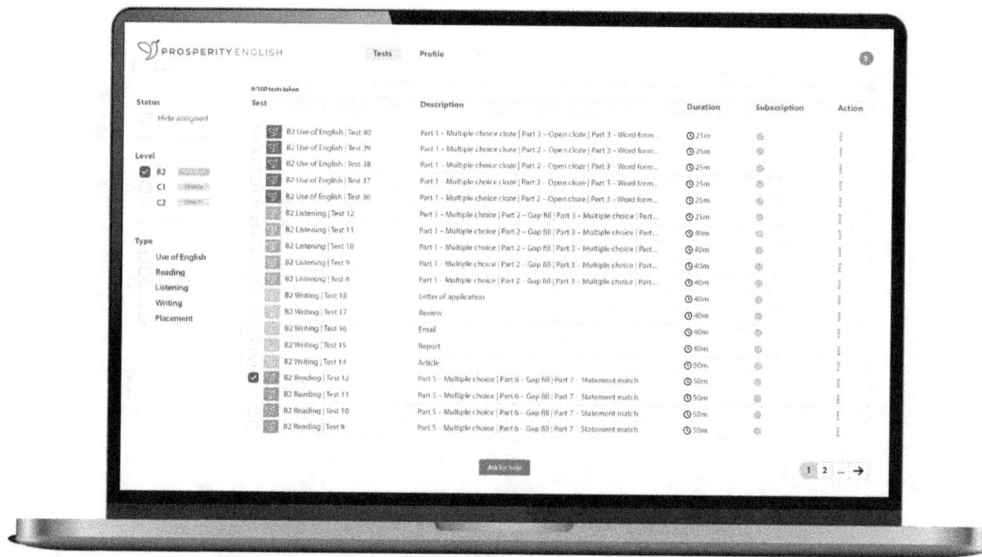

Prosperity English provides ample opportunities for repetitive practice, allowing you to reinforce your learning and improve your exam skills steadily.

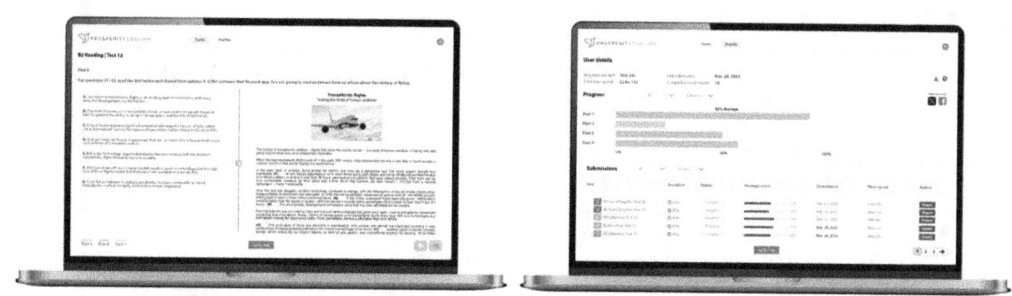

Try it for free

www.prosperityenglish.com

40% promotional discount code:
TIAB40

Contents

Introduction	*v*
Test 1	*1*
Test 2	*9*
Test 3	*17*
Test 4	*25*
Test 5	*33*
Test 6	*41*
Test 7	*49*
Test 8	*57*
Test 9	*65*
Test 10	*73*
Bonus content: B2 Speaking practice test + model answers	*81*

How to download the colour Part 2 booklet:

1. Go to www.prosperityeducation.net
2. Select the Downloads page
3. Select the book cover image
4. Download the .pdf content

Introduction

Welcome to this edition of sample tests for the Cambridge B1 Preliminary Speaking, which has been written to replicate the Cambridge exam experience and has undergone rigorous expert and peer review.

The B1 Preliminary English language exam is the third of six levels established in the Common European Framework of Reference (CEFR): A1–C2. Candidates of all ages can take the B1 Preliminary test. In the exam you will have approximately 25 minutes to complete the Speaking paper. This section has four parts, and is worth 25% of the final score.

This section of the exam is taken in pairs of candidates, who are assessed by two examiners: the interlocutor and the assessor. The interlocutor is responsible for delivering the instructions, handling the test booklet and interacting with the candidates, while the assessor simply listens and marks each candidate's performance.

The Speaking paper is divided into four parts, all of which comprise a different task. Different degrees of participation are expected from the candidates in each of these tasks.

	Timing	Interaction	Task types	What do candidates have to do?
Part 1	2 minutes	Interlocutor Candidate	Interlocutor asks questions to each candidate in turn	Respond to questions, giving factual or personal information.
Part 2	3 minutes	Candidate extended turn	Extended turn	Describe one colour photograph, talking for about 1 minute.
Part 3	4 minutes	Candidate Candidate	Discussion task with visual stimulus	Make and respond to suggestions, discuss alternatives and negotiate agreement.
Part 4	3 minutes	Candidate Candidate	General conversation	Discuss likes, dislikes, experiences, opinions, habits, etc.
Total	25			

For more information, visit the Cambridge Assessment English website.

This book contains 10 Speaking tests (Parts 1–4). You or your students, if you are a teacher, will hopefully enjoy the wide range of tasks and benefit from the repetitive practice, something that is key to preparing for this part of the B1 Preliminary (PET) examination.

Included as bonus material at the end of the book is a B2 Speaking practice test with model answers.

We hope that you will find this resource a useful study aid, and wish you all the best in preparing for the exam.

Cambridge B1 Preliminary

Speaking

Test 1

© 2025 Prosperity Education.
'Cambridge B1 Preliminary' and 'PET' are brands belonging to The Chancellor, Masters and Scholars of the University of Cambridge and are not associated with Prosperity Education or its products.

Speaking B1 | Ten tests for the Cambridge Preliminary

Speaking Test 1 — Part 1 (2–3 minutes)

Phase 1

Interlocutor

To both candidates
Good morning / afternoon / evening.
Can I have your mark sheets, please?
Hand over the mark sheets to the Assessor.
I'm .... and this is ....

To Candidate A
What's your name? How old are you?
Thank you.

To Candidate B
And what's your name? How old are you?
Thank you.

	Back-up prompts
B, where do you live?	Do you live in *name of town, city or region*?
	Do you live in a house or a flat?
Who do you live with?	Do you live with your family?
	How many people do you live with?
Thank you.	
And **A**, where do you live?	Do you live in *name of town, city or region*?
	Do you live in a house or a flat?
Who do you live with?	Do you live with your family?
	How many people do you live with?
Thank you.	

Phase 2

Interlocutor

Select one or more questions from the list to ask each candidate.

Ask Candidate A first.

	Back-up prompts
Where do you usually go on holiday?	Do you go to another country on holiday? (Why?/Why not?)
How often do you go on a train?	Do you often go on a train? (Why?/Why not?)
Tell us about a subject you like at school. (Why?)	Which school subject do you like most?
Which do you prefer, rock music or classical music? (Why?)	Which is better, rock music or classical music? (Why?)

Thank you.

Speaking B1 | Ten tests for the Cambridge Preliminary

Speaking Test 1   Part 2 (2–3 minutes)

1A Doing a hobby

Interlocutor	Now I'd like each of you to talk on your own about something. I'm going to give each of you a photograph and I'd like you to talk about it.
	A, here is your photograph. It shows **someone doing a hobby**.
	*Place **Part 2** booklet, open at **Task 1A**, in front of candidate.*
	B, you just listen.
	A, please tell us what you can see in the photograph.
Candidate A	
⏱ *approx. 1 minute*	…………………………………………………………………………
	Back-up prompts • Talk about the people/person. • Talk about the place. • Talk about other things in the photograph.
Interlocutor	Thank you. (Can I have the booklet please?) *Retrieve **Part 2** booklet.*

1B Having a meal

Interlocutor	**B**, here is your photograph. It shows **some people having a meal**.
	*Place **Part 2** booklet, open at **Task 1B**, in front of candidate.*
	A, you just listen.
	B, please tell us what you can see in the photograph.
Candidate B	
⏱ *approx. 1 minute*	…………………………………………………………………………
	Back-up prompts • Talk about the people/person. • Talk about the place. • Talk about other things in the photograph.
Interlocutor	Thank you. (Can I have the booklet please?) *Retrieve **Part 2** booklet.*

Test 1

1A

1B

Speaking B1 | Ten tests for the Cambridge Preliminary

Speaking Test 1 (Activities for the weekend)

Parts 3 and 4 (6 minutes)

Part 3

Interlocutor Now, in this part of the test you're going to talk about something together for about two minutes. I'm going to describe a situation to you.

*Place **Part 3** booklet, open at **Task 1**, in front of the candidates.*

Some friends are choosing an activity for the weekend.

Here are some activities they could do.

Talk together about the different activities they could do, and say which would be most interesting.

All right? Now, talk together.

Candidates ....

⏲ *approx. 2–3 minutes*

Interlocutor Thank you. (Can I have the booklet please?) *Retrieve **Part 3** booklet.*

Part 4

Interlocutor *Use the following questions, as appropriate:*

- **Which activities would you not like to do at the weekend? (Why not?)**
- **Do you prefer indoor or outdoor activities at the weekend? (Why?)**
- **Do you enjoy activities that are done on water? (Why?/Why not?)**
- **Which activities can you do in your town or city at the weekend?**
- **Which do you think is more interesting: doing an activity on your own or with friends? (Why?)**

Select any of the following prompts, as appropriate:
- **How/what about you?**
- **Do you agree?**
- **What do you think?**

Thank you. That is the end of the test.

Activities for the weekend

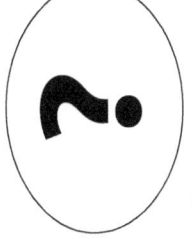

Cambridge B1 Preliminary

Speaking

Test 2

© 2025 Prosperity Education.
'Cambridge B1 Preliminary' and 'PET' are brands belonging to The Chancellor, Masters and Scholars of the University of Cambridge and are not associated with Prosperity Education or its products.

Speaking B1 | Ten tests for the Cambridge Preliminary

Speaking Test 2   Part 1 (2–3 minutes)

Phase 1

Interlocutor

To both candidates   Good morning / afternoon / evening.
                        Can I have your mark sheets, please?
                        Hand over the mark sheets to the Assessor.
                        I'm .... and this is ....

To Candidate A   What's your name? How old are you?
                        Thank you.

To Candidate B   And what's your name? How old are you?
                        Thank you.

	Back-up prompts
B, how old are you?	When is your birthday?
	Do you usually have a birthday party?
How many brothers	Do you have a big family?
and sisters do you have?	How many people do you live with?
Thank you.	
A, how old are you?	When is your birthday?
	Do you usually have a birthday party?
How many brothers	Do you have a big family?
and sisters do you have?	How many people do you live with?
Thank you.	

Phase 2

Interlocutor

Select one or more questions from the list to ask each candidate.

Ask Candidate A first.

	Back-up prompts
How often do you watch television?	Do you often watch television on your own? (Why?/Why not?)
Do you watch television in your bedroom? (Why?/Why not?)	Where do you watch television?
How do you usually spend your weekends?	Do you go out with your friends at the weekend? (Why not?)
Which kind of clothes do you prefer?	Do you buy a lot of clothes? (Why?/Why not?)
Tell us about a sport you like.	Which sport do you like? (Why?)

Thank you.

Speaking Test 2 — Part 2 (2–3 minutes)

1A Learning a sport

Interlocutor

Now I'd like each of you to talk on your own about something. I'm going to give each of you a photograph and I'd like you to talk about it.

A, here is your photograph. It shows **someone learning a sport**.

Place Part 2 booklet, open at Task 1A, in front of candidate.

B, you just listen.

A, please tell us what you can see in the photograph.

Candidate A

⏱ approx. 1 minute

....

Back-up prompts
- Talk about the people/person.
- Talk about the place.
- Talk about other things in the photograph.

Interlocutor

Thank you. (Can I have the booklet please?) *Retrieve Part 2 booklet.*

1B Shopping

Interlocutor

B, here is your photograph. It shows **some people shopping**.

Place Part 2 booklet, open at Task 1B, in front of candidate.

A, you just listen.

B, please tell us what you can see in the photograph.

Candidate B

⏱ approx. 1 minute

....

Back-up prompts
- Talk about the people/person.
- Talk about the place.
- Talk about other things in the photograph.

Interlocutor

Thank you. (Can I have the booklet please?) *Retrieve Part 2 booklet.*

1A

1B

Speaking Test 2 (Hobbies and interests)

Parts 3 and 4 (6 minutes)

Part 3

Interlocutor Now, in this part of the test you're going to talk about something together for about two minutes. I'm going to describe a situation to you.

Place Part 3 booklet, open at Task 1, in front of the candidates.

A teenager is bored in her free time. She wants to take up a new hobby or interest.

Here are some hobbies and interests she could take up.

Talk together about the different activities and say which would be most interesting.

All right? Now, talk together.

Candidates ……………………………………………………..

⏲ approx. 2–3 minutes

Interlocutor Thank you. (Can I have the booklet please?) *Retrieve Part 3 booklet.*

Part 4

Interlocutor *Use the following questions, as appropriate:*

- **Which hobbies would you like to take up? (Why?)**
- **Do you enjoy hobbies that involve creating or making things? (Why?/Why not?)**
- **Do you prefer indoor or outdoor hobbies? (Why?)**
- **Which hobbies can't you do in your town or city? (Why not?)**
- **Which do you think is more interesting: doing a hobby on your own or with friends? (Why?)**

Select any of the following prompts, as appropriate:
- **How/what about you?**
- **Do you agree?**
- **What do you think?**

Thank you. That is the end of the test.

Hobbies and interests

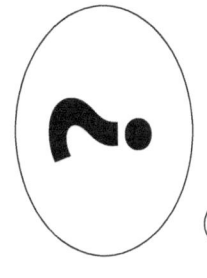

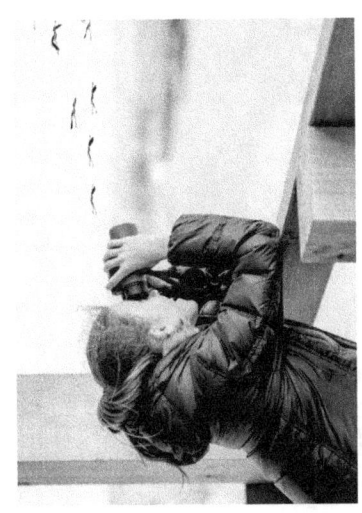

Cambridge B1 Preliminary

Speaking

Test 3

© 2025 Prosperity Education.
'Cambridge B1 Preliminary' and 'PET' are brands belonging to The Chancellor, Masters and Scholars of the University of Cambridge and are not associated with Prosperity Education or its products.

Speaking Test 3

Part 1 (2–3 minutes)

Phase 1

Interlocutor

To both candidates

Good morning / afternoon / evening.
Can I have your mark sheets, please?
Hand over the mark sheets to the Assessor.
I'm ………… and this is ………… .

To Candidate A

What's your name? How old are you?
Thank you.

To Candidate B

And what's your name? How old are you?
Thank you.

	Back-up prompts
B, do you have a big family?	How many brothers and sisters have you got? Do your grandparents live with you?
What activities do you and your family do together?	Do you spend a lot of time with your grandparents? What activities do you do with your brothers and sisters?
Thank you.	
And **A**, do you have a big family?	How many brothers and sisters have you got? Do your grandparents live with you?
What activities do you and your family do together?	Do you spend a lot of time with your grandparents? What activities do you do with your brothers and sisters?
Thank you.	

Phase 2

Interlocutor

Select one or more questions from the list to ask each candidate.

Ask Candidate A first.

	Back-up prompts
Tell us about a kind of food you like.	What do you like to eat for lunch or dinner? (Why?)
How often do you go to the cinema?	Do you often go to the cinema? (Why?/Why not?) When did you last go to the cinema? What did you see?
How do you usually travel to school?	Do you ever cycle to school? (Why?/Why not?)
Which do you prefer, hot drinks or cold drinks? (Why?)	Which is better, tea, coffee or juice? (Why?)

Thank you.

Speaking Test 3

Part 2 (2–3 minutes)

1A Doing jobs around the house

Interlocutor Now I'd like each of you to talk on your own about something. I'm going to give each of you a photograph and I'd like you to talk about it.

A, here is your photograph. It shows **someone doing jobs around the house**.

Place Part 2 booklet, open at Task 1A, in front of candidate.

B, you just listen.

A, please tell us what you can see in the photograph.

Candidate A

⏲ approx. 1 minute

....

Back-up prompts
- Talk about the people/person.
- Talk about the place.
- Talk about other things in the photograph.

Interlocutor Thank you. (Can I have the booklet please?) *Retrieve Part 2 booklet.*

1B Playing computer games

Interlocutor B, here is your photograph. It shows **someone playing a computer game**.

Place Part 2 booklet, open at Task 1B, in front of candidate.

A, you just listen.

B, please tell us what you can see in the photograph.

Candidate B

⏲ approx. 1 minute

....

Back-up prompts
- Talk about the people/person.
- Talk about the place.
- Talk about other things in the photograph.

Interlocutor Thank you. (Can I have the booklet please?) *Retrieve Part 2 booklet.*

Speaking Test 3 (Jobs)

Parts 3 and 4 (6 minutes)

Part 3

Interlocutor Now, in this part of the test you're going to talk about something together for about two minutes. I'm going to describe a situation to you.
Place Part 3 booklet, open at Task 1, in front of the candidates.
Some friends are talking about jobs they could do when they finish their education.
Here are some jobs they could do.
Talk together about the different jobs they could do, and say which would be most interesting.
All right? Now, talk together.

Candidates ....

⏲ *approx. 2–3 minutes*

Interlocutor Thank you. (Can I have the booklet please?) *Retrieve Part 3 booklet.*

Part 4

Interlocutor *Use the following questions, as appropriate:*
- **Which jobs would you not like to do? (Why?)**
- **Which jobs do you think you would most enjoy doing? (Why?)**
- **Do you prefer indoor or outdoor jobs? (Why?)**
- **Which jobs have a good wage in your country? (Why?)**
- **Which do you think is more important: doing an interesting job or doing a job with a good wage? (Why?)**

Select any of the following prompts, as appropriate:
- **How/what about you?**
- **Do you agree?**
- **What do you think?**

Thank you. That is the end of the test.

Jobs

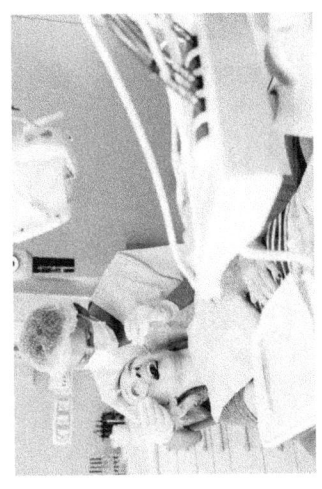

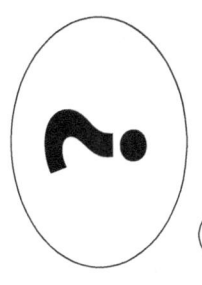

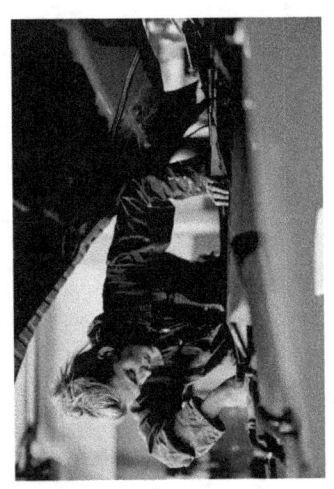

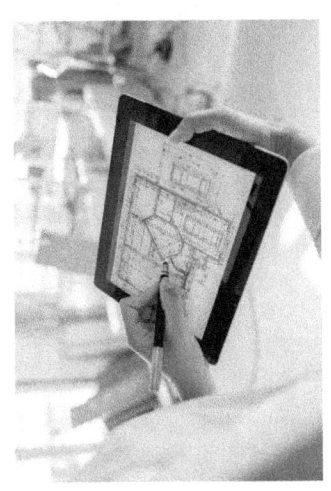

Cambridge B1 Preliminary

Speaking

Test 4

Speaking Test 4 — Part 1 (2–3 minutes)

Phase 1

Interlocutor

To both candidates
Good morning / afternoon / evening.
Can I have your mark sheets, please?
Hand over the mark sheets to the Assessor.
I'm .... and this is ....

To Candidate A
What's your name? How old are you?
Thank you.

To Candidate B
And what's your name? How old are you?
Thank you.

	Back-up prompts
B, which school do you go to?	Is your school big or small?
	Do you like your school? (Why?/Why not?)
Where do you live?	Do you live in a house or a flat?
	Do you live close to your school?
Thank you.	
And **A**, which school do you go to?	Is your school big or small?
	Do you like your school? (Why?/Why not?)
Where do you live?	Do you live in a house or a flat?
	Do you live close to your school?
Thank you.	

Phase 2

Interlocutor

Select one or more questions from the list to ask each candidate.

Ask Candidate A first.

	Back-up prompts
How often do you go to a restaurant?	Do you often go to a restaurant? (Why?/Why not?)
	When did you last go to a restaurant? What did you eat and drink?
What do you usually do after school?	Do you go straight home? (Why?/Why not?)
Which do you prefer, fiction books or books about facts? (Why?)	What are you reading at the moment? (Why?)
Tell us about a place you like to visit.	Where do you like to go at the weekend? (Why?)

Thank you.

Speaking Test 4 — Part 2 (2–3 minutes)

1A Watching a TV programme

Interlocutor: Now I'd like each of you to talk on your own about something. I'm going to give each of you a photograph and I'd like you to talk about it.

A, here is your photograph. It shows **some people watching a TV programme**.

Place Part 2 booklet, open at Task 1A, in front of candidate.

B, you just listen.

A, please tell us what you can see in the photograph.

Candidate A

⏱ approx. 1 minute

....

> **Back-up prompts**
> - Talk about the people/person.
> - Talk about the place.
> - Talk about other things in the photograph.

Interlocutor: Thank you. (Can I have the booklet please?) *Retrieve Part 2 booklet.*

1B Cycling

Interlocutor: B, here is your photograph. It shows **some people cycling**.

Place Part 2 booklet, open at Task 1B, in front of candidate.

A, you just listen.

B, please tell us what you can see in the photograph.

Candidate B

⏱ approx. 1 minute

....

> **Back-up prompts**
> - Talk about the people/person.
> - Talk about the place.
> - Talk about other things in the photograph.

Interlocutor: Thank you. (Can I have the booklet please?) *Retrieve Part 2 booklet.*

Speaking Test 4 (Holidays)

Parts 3 and 4 (6 minutes)

Part 3

Interlocutor Now, in this part of the test you're going to talk about something together for about two minutes. I'm going to describe a situation to you.
Place Part 3 booklet, open at Task 1, in front of the candidates.
A family is choosing a type of holiday for the summer.
Here are some types of holiday they could go on.
Talk together about the different holidays they could go on, and say which would be the most interesting.
All right? Now, talk together.

Candidates ....

⏱ *approx. 2–3 minutes*

Interlocutor Thank you. (Can I have the booklet please?) *Retrieve Part 3 booklet.*

Part 4

Interlocutor *Use the following questions, as appropriate:*
- **Which types of holidays would you not like to go on? (Why?)**
- **What do you need to take with you for holidays?**
- **Do you prefer a quiet holiday or a holiday with lots of activities? (Why?)**
- **Which types of holidays can you do easily from your town or city? (Why?)**
- **Which do you think is more interesting: going on holiday with your family or with friends? (Why?)**

Select any of the following prompts, as appropriate:
- **How/what about you?**
- **Do you agree?**
- **What do you think?**

Thank you. That is the end of the test.

Holidays

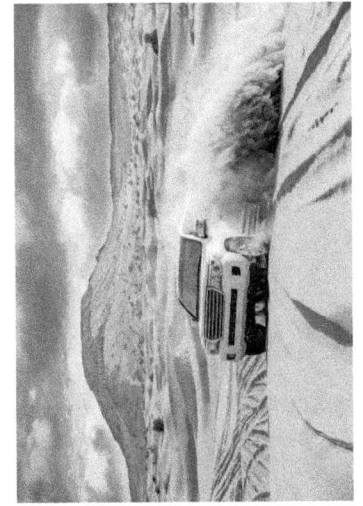

Cambridge B1 Preliminary

Speaking

Test 5

Speaking Test 5 — Part 1 (2–3 minutes)

Phase 1

Interlocutor

To both candidates
Good morning / afternoon / evening.
Can I have your mark sheets, please?
Hand over the mark sheets to the Assessor.
I'm .... and this is ....

To Candidate A
What's your name? How old are you?
Thank you.

To Candidate B
And what's your name? How old are you?
Thank you.

	Back-up prompts
B, what do you do in your free time?	What do you do at the weekend?
	What are your hobbies?
How many brothers and sisters do you have?	Do you have any brothers (sisters)?
	What about sisters (brothers)?
	Are they older or younger than you?
Thank you.	
And **A**, what do you do in your free time?	What do you do at the weekend?
	What are your hobbies?
How many brothers and sisters do you have?	Do you have any brothers (sisters)?
	What about sisters (brothers)?
	Are they older or younger than you?
Thank you.	

Phase 2

Interlocutor

Select one or more questions from the list to ask each candidate.

Ask Candidate A first.

	Back-up prompts
How often do you go on social media?	Do you often use social media like Facebook? (Why?/Why not?) When did you last go onto social media? (Why?)
How do you help around the house?	Do you keep your room tidy? (Why?/Why not?) Do you help with the washing-up? (Why?/Why not?)
Which do you prefer, cats or dogs? (Why?)	Have you got a pet? (Why?/Why not?)
Tell us about a teacher you like.	Which teacher do you like? (Why?)

Thank you.

Speaking Test 5 — Part 2 (2–3 minutes)

1A Doing an experiment

Interlocutor: Now I'd like each of you to talk on your own about something. I'm going to give each of you a photograph and I'd like you to talk about it.

A, here is your photograph. It shows **some children doing an experiment**.

Place Part 2 booklet, open at Task 1A, in front of candidate.

B, you just listen.

A, please tell us what you can see in the photograph.

Candidate A
⏲ approx. 1 minute ....

Back-up prompts
- Talk about the people/person.
- Talk about the place.
- Talk about other things in the photograph.

Interlocutor: Thank you. (Can I have the booklet please?) *Retrieve Part 2 booklet.*

1B Using smartphones

Interlocutor: B, here is your photograph. It shows **some people using their smartphones**.

Place Part 2 booklet, open at Task 1B, in front of candidate.

A, you just listen.

B, please tell us what you can see in the photograph.

Candidate B
⏲ approx. 1 minute ....

Back-up prompts
- Talk about the people/person.
- Talk about the place.
- Talk about other things in the photograph.

Interlocutor: Thank you. (Can I have the booklet please?) *Retrieve Part 2 booklet.*

Test 5

1A

1B

Speaking Test 5 (Sports and games)

Parts 3 and 4 (6 minutes)

Part 3

Interlocutor Now, in this part of the test you're going to talk about something together for about two minutes. I'm going to describe a situation to you.

*Place **Part 3** booklet, open at **Task 1**, in front of the candidates.*

A boy loves sport and wants to learn a new sport.

Here are some sports he could learn.

Talk together about the different sports the boy could do, and say which would be most interesting.

All right? Now, talk together.

Candidates ....

⏱ *approx. 2–3 minutes*

Interlocutor Thank you. (Can I have the booklet please?) *Retrieve **Part 3** booklet.*

Part 4

Interlocutor *Use the following questions, as appropriate:*

- **Which sports can you play? How good are you?**
- **Do you prefer to play indoor sports or outdoor sports? (Why?)**
- **Do you prefer team sports like football, or individual sports like skiing? (Why?)**
- **Which sports can you do easily in your town or city? (Why?)**
- **Which do you think is more interesting: practising a sport or playing it in a game or match? (Why?)**

> *Select any of the following prompts, as appropriate:*
> - **How/what about you?**
> - **Do you agree?**
> - **What do you think?**

Thank you. That is the end of the test.

Sports and games

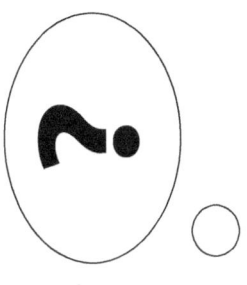

Cambridge B1 Preliminary

Speaking

Test 6

© 2025 Prosperity Education.
'Cambridge B1 Preliminary' and 'PET' are brands belonging to The Chancellor, Masters and Scholars of the University of Cambridge and are not associated with Prosperity Education or its products.

Speaking Test 6

Part 1 (2–3 minutes)

Phase 1

Interlocutor

To both candidates	Good morning / afternoon / evening.
	Can I have your mark sheets, please?
	Hand over the mark sheets to the Assessor.
	I'm ………… and this is ………… .
To Candidate A	What's your name? How old are you?
	Thank you.
To Candidate B	And what's your name? How old are you?
	Thank you.

	Back-up prompts
B, where do you live?	Do you live in a house or a flat?
	Is it big or small?
Where do you go to school?	Do you like your school?
	Can you walk to school?
Thank you.	
And **A**, where do you live?	Do you live in a house or a flat?
	Is it big or small?
Where do you go to school?	Do you like your school?
	Can you walk to school?
Thank you.	

Phase 2

Interlocutor

Select one or more questions from the list to ask each candidate.

Ask Candidate A first.

	Back-up prompts
How often do you play sport?	Do you often play sport? (Why?/Why not?) What's your favourite sport?
Where do you usually go on holiday?	Do you go to another country? (Why?/Why not?)
Which do you prefer, meat, fis or vegetables?	Which is better, meat or fish? Why?)
Tell us about a film ou like.	What is the best part of the film? Why?)

Thank you.

Speaking Test 6 — Part 2 (2–3 minutes)

1A Learning to drive

Interlocutor Now I'd like each of you to talk on your own about something. I'm going to give each of you a photograph and I'd like you to talk about it.

A, here is your photograph. It shows **a person learning to drive**.

Place Part 2 booklet, open at Task 1A, in front of candidate.

B, you just listen.

A, please tell us what you can see in the photograph.

Candidate A

⏱ *approx. 1 minute* ....

Back-up prompts
- Talk about the people/person.
- Talk about the place.
- Talk about other things in the photograph.

Interlocutor Thank you. (Can I have the booklet please?) *Retrieve Part 2 booklet.*

1B Doing a hobby

Interlocutor **B**, here is your photograph. It shows **some people doing a hobby**.

Place Part 2 booklet, open at Task 1B, in front of candidate.

A, you just listen.

B, please tell us what you can see in the photograph.

Candidate B

⏱ *approx. 1 minute* ....

Back-up prompts
- Talk about the people/person.
- Talk about the place.
- Talk about other things in the photograph.

Interlocutor Thank you. (Can I have the booklet please?) *Retrieve Part 2 booklet.*

Speaking Test 6 (Evening activities)

Parts 3 and 4 (6 minutes)

Part 3

Interlocutor Now, in this part of the test you're going to talk about something together for about two minutes. I'm going to describe a situation to you.

Place Part 3 booklet, open at Task 1, in front of the candidates.

Some friends are choosing somewhere to go this evening.

Here are some places they could go.

Talk together about the different places, and say which would be most interesting.

All right? Now, talk together.

Candidates ……………………………………………………..

⏱ *approx. 2–3 minutes*

Interlocutor Thank you. (Can I have the booklet please?) *Retrieve Part 3 booklet.*

Part 4

Interlocutor *Use the following questions, as appropriate:*

- **Where do you like to go in the evenings? (Why?)**
- **Do you do different evening activities during the week and at weekends? (Why?)**
- **Do you prefer to spend the evening indoors or outdoors? (Why?)**
- **Who do you usually do evening activities with? (Why?)**
- **Which do you think is more interesting: going to a film or going to a music concert? (Why?)**

Select any of the following prompts, as appropriate:
- **How/what about you?**
- **Do you agree?**
- **What do you think?**

Thank you. **That is the end of the test.**

Evening activities

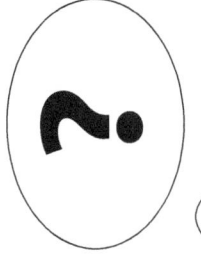

Cambridge B1 Preliminary

Speaking

Test 7

© 2025 Prosperity Education.
'Cambridge B1 Preliminary' and 'PET' are brands belonging to The Chancellor, Masters and Scholars of the University of Cambridge and are not associated with Prosperity Education or its products.

Speaking Test 7

Part 1 (2–3 minutes)

Phase 1

Interlocutor

To both candidates Good morning / afternoon / evening.
Can I have your mark sheets, please?
Hand over the mark sheets to the Assessor.
I'm .... and this is ....

To Candidate A What's your name? How old are you?
Thank you.

To Candidate B And what's your name? How old are you?
Thank you.

	Back-up prompts
B, where do you live?	What is the name of your town or city? Is it big or small?
What are the best things about the place you live in?	What's your favourite thing about your town or city?
Where do you go to in your town or city at the weekend? Thank you.	
And **A**, where do you live?	What is the name of your town or city? Is it big or small?
What are the best things about the place you live in? Thank you.	What's your favourite thing about your town or city? Where do you go to in your town or city at the weekend?

Phase 2

Interlocutor

Select one or more questions from the list to ask each candidate.

Ask Candidate A first.

	Back-up prompts
How often do you watch television?	Do you watch television on your own? (Why?/Why not?) Do you watch television in your bedroom? What do you watch on television?
How do you usually get to school?	Do you ever walk / go by bus / go on the train? (Why not?)
Tell us about the books you like.	Which type of books do you like? (Why?)
Which kind of sports do you prefer?	Do you like team sports? (Why?/Why not?)

Thank you.

Speaking Test 7

Part 2 (2–3 minutes)

1A Playing a computer game

Interlocutor	Now I'd like each of you to talk on your own about something. I'm going to give each of you a photograph and I'd like you to talk about it. **A**, here is your photograph. It shows **someone playing a computer game**. *Place **Part 2** booklet, open at **Task 1A**, in front of candidate.* **B**, you just listen. **A**, please tell us what you can see in the photograph.
Candidate A ⏲ approx. 1 minute	……………………………………………………………… **Back-up prompts** • Talk about the people/person. • Talk about the place. • Talk about other things in the photograph.
Interlocutor	Thank you. (Can I have the booklet please?) *Retrieve **Part 2** booklet.*

1B At the beach

Interlocutor	**B**, here is your photograph. It shows **some people at the beach**. *Place **Part 2** booklet, open at **Task 1B**, in front of candidate.* **A**, you just listen. **B**, please tell us what you can see in the photograph.
Candidate B ⏲ approx. 1 minute	……………………………………………………………… **Back-up prompts** • Talk about the people/person. • Talk about the place. • Talk about other things in the photograph.
Interlocutor	Thank you. (Can I have the booklet please?) *Retrieve **Part 2** booklet.*

1A

1B

Speaking Test 7 (After-school clubs)

Parts 3 and 4 (6 minutes)

Part 3

Interlocutor Now, in this part of the test you're going to talk about something together for about two minutes. I'm going to describe a situation to you.
Place Part 3 booklet, open at Task 1, in front of the candidates.
A teenager wants to go to an after-school club.
Here are some clubs she could go to.
Talk together about the different clubs, and say which would be most interesting.
All right? Now, talk together.

Candidates ……………………………………………………..

⏱ *approx. 2–3 minutes*

Interlocutor Thank you. (Can I have the booklet please?) *Retrieve Part 3 booklet.*

Part 4

Interlocutor *Use the following questions, as appropriate:*
- **What are your favourite after-school clubs? (Why?)**
- **Do you think all young people should go to after-school cubs? (Why?)**
- **Do you prefer indoor or outdoor clubs? (Why?)**
- **What after-school clubs have you got at your school?**
- **Which do you think is more interesting: a hobby club or a sports club? (Why?)**

Select any of the following prompts, as appropriate:
- **How/what about you?**
- **Do you agree?**
- **What do you think?**

Thank you. **That is the end of the test.**

After-school clubs

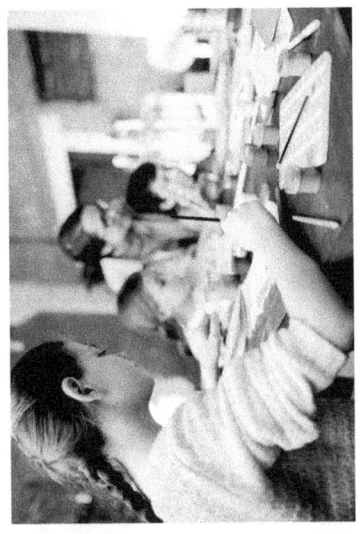
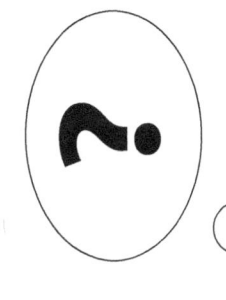

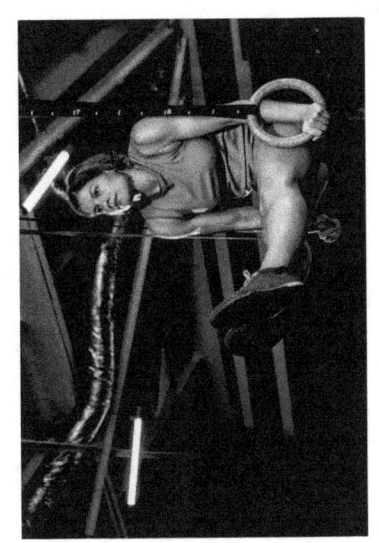

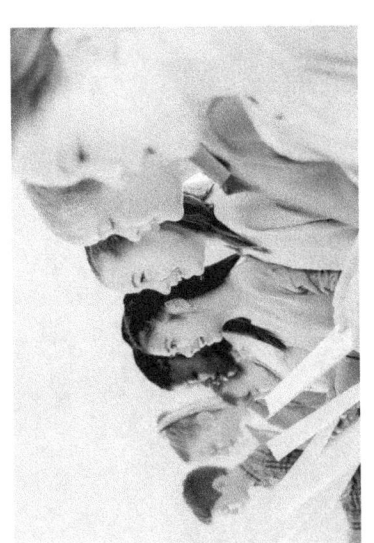

Cambridge B1 Preliminary

Speaking

Test 8

© 2025 Prosperity Education.
'Cambridge B1 Preliminary' and 'PET' are brands belonging to The Chancellor, Masters and Scholars of the University of Cambridge and are not associated with Prosperity Education or its products.

Speaking Test 8 — Part 1 (2–3 minutes)

Phase 1

Interlocutor

To both candidates

Good morning / afternoon / evening.
Can I have your mark sheets, please?
Hand over the mark sheets to the Assessor.
I'm .... and this is ....

To Candidate A

What's your name? How old are you?
Thank you.

To Candidate B

And what's your name? How old are you?
Thank you.

	Back-up prompts
B, when is your birthday?	Is your birthday this month?
	Do you always have a party?
Where do you live?	Do you live in a house or a flat?
	Is it near the centre of the town or city?
Thank you.	
And **A**, when is your birthday?	Is your birthday this month?
	Do you always have a party?
Where do you live?	Do you live in a house or a flat?
	Is it near the centre of the town or city?
Thank you.	

Phase 2

Interlocutor

Select one or more questions from the list to ask each candidate.

Ask Candidate A first.

	Back-up prompts
How often do you go to another country?	Have you been to many other countries? (Why?/Why not?)
	Is it easy to get to other countries? (Why?/Why not?)
	Where would you like to visit? (Why?)
Have you got any pets?	What pets have you got?
	OR
	Would you like to have a pet? (Why?/Why not?)
Which kind of clothes do you prefer?	Do you like T-shirts and jeans? (Why?/Why not?)
Tell us about a board game you like – (Why?) for example, chess.	Which type of board games do you like?

Thank you.

Speaking Test 8

Part 2 (2–3 minutes)

1A Online learning

Interlocutor	Now I'd like each of you to talk on your own about something. I'm going to give each of you a photograph and I'd like you to talk about it. **A**, here is your photograph. It shows **someone learning online**. *Place Part 2 booklet, open at Task 1A, in front of candidate.* **B**, you just listen. **A**, please tell us what you can see in the photograph.
Candidate A ⏱ *approx. 1 minute*	....
	Back-up prompts • Talk about the people/person. • Talk about the place. • Talk about other things in the photograph.
Interlocutor	Thank you. (Can I have the booklet please?) *Retrieve Part 2 booklet.*

1B Playing music

Interlocutor	**B**, here is your photograph. It shows **some people playing music**. *Place Part 2 booklet, open at Task 1B, in front of candidate.* **A**, you just listen. **B**, please tell us what you can see in the photograph.
Candidate B ⏱ *approx. 1 minute*	....
	Back-up prompts • Talk about the people/person. • Talk about the place. • Talk about other things in the photograph.
Interlocutor	Thank you. (Can I have the booklet please?) *Retrieve Part 2 booklet.*

Speaking Test 8 (Fast food)

Parts 3 and 4 (6 minutes)

Part 3

Interlocutor Now, in this part of the test you're going to talk about something together for about two minutes. I'm going to describe a situation to you.

Place Part 3 booklet, open at Task 1, in front of the candidates.

A teenager wants to order some food online for a meal at his house. Here are some types of food he could order.

Talk together about the different types of food, and say which would be the best for him/her.

All right? Now, talk together.

Candidates ....

⏲ *approx. 2–3 minutes*

Interlocutor Thank you. (Can I have the booklet please?) *Retrieve Part 3 booklet.*

Part 4

Interlocutor *Use the following questions, as appropriate:*

- **What is your favourite meal? (Why?)**
- **Are there any types of food you won't eat?**
- **Do you prefer fast food or meals in a restaurant? (Why?)**
- **What types of restaurant are there near to where you live?**
- **Which do you think is best: a restaurant meal or a home-cooked meal? (Why?)**

Select any of the following prompts, as appropriate:
- **How/what about you?**
- **Do you agree?**
- **What do you think?**

Thank you. **That is the end of the test.**

Fast food

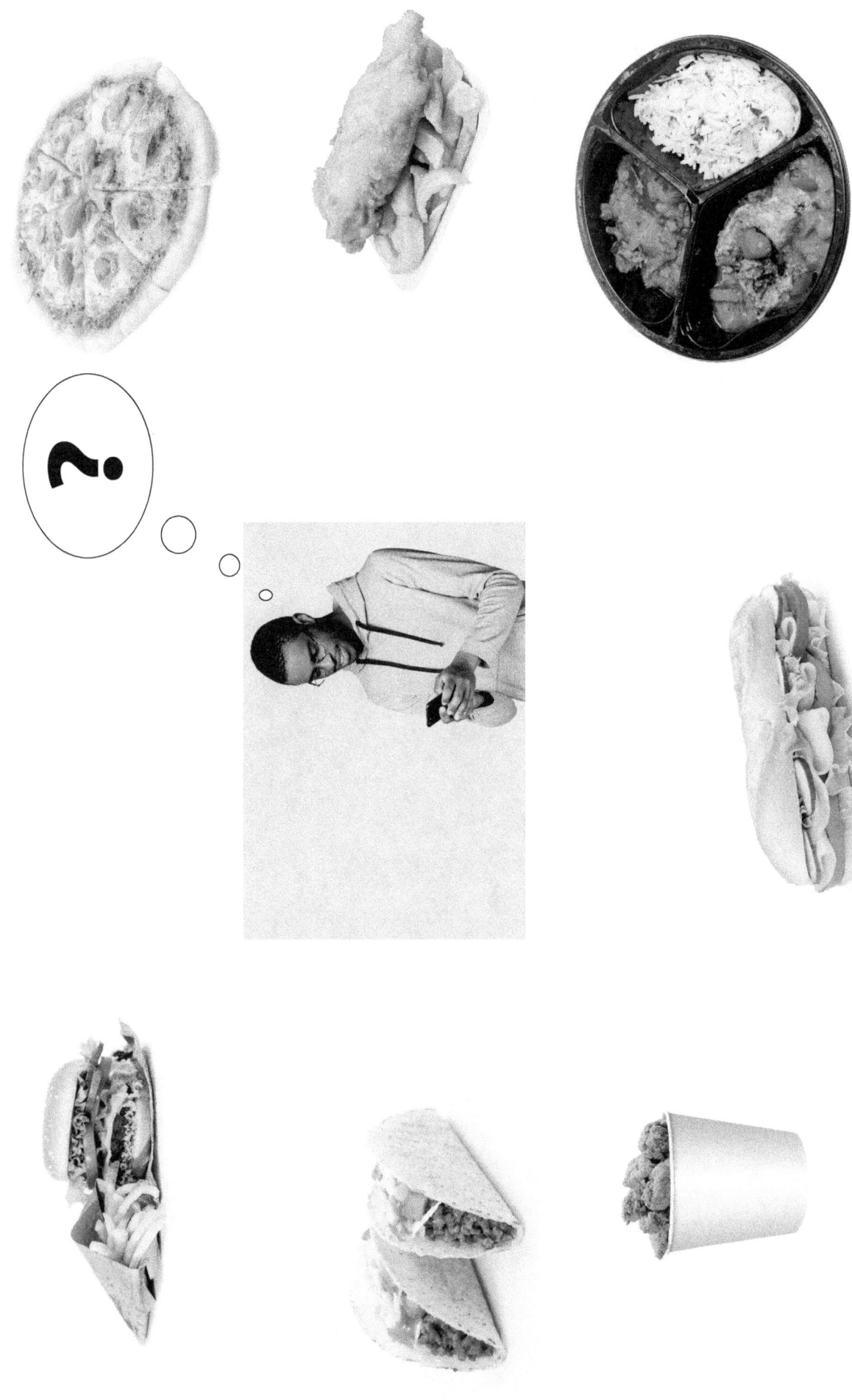

Cambridge B1 Preliminary

Speaking

Test 9

Speaking Test 9

Part 1 (2–3 minutes)

Phase 1

Interlocutor

To both candidates	Good morning / afternoon / evening.
	Can I have your mark sheets, please?
	Hand over the mark sheets to the Assessor.
	I'm .... and this is ....
To Candidate A	What's your name? How old are you?
	Thank you.
To Candidate B	And what's your name? How old are you?
	Thank you.

	Back-up prompts
B, where do you live?	Do you live in a village, a town or a city?
	Do you live in a house or a flat?
Where do you go to school?	Is your school close to your house?
	Is it a big school or a small school?
Thank you.	
And **A**, where do you live?	Do you live in a village, a town or a city?
	Do you live in a house or a flat?
Where do you go to school?	Is your school close to your house?
	Is it a big school or a small school?
Thank you.	

Phase 2

Interlocutor

Select one or more questions from the list to ask each candidate.

Ask Candidate A first.

	Back-up prompts
How often do you eat fast food?	Do you often eat fast food? (Why?/Why not?) When did you last have a fast-food meal? What did you have?
How do you get to school?	Do you go to school by bus? (Why?/Why not?)
How much do you help around the house?	What are you reading at the moment? (Why?)
Tell us about a sport that you like.	Do you make your bed or clean your room? (Why not?)
Thank you.	

Speaking Test 9 — Part 2 (2–3 minutes)

1A Doing a hobby

Interlocutor	Now I'd like each of you to talk on your own about something. I'm going to give each of you a photograph and I'd like you to talk about it. **A**, here is your photograph. It shows **a person doing a hobby**. *Place **Part 2** booklet, open at **Task 1A**, in front of candidate.* **B**, you just listen. **A**, please tell us what you can see in the photograph.
Candidate A ⏲ approx. 1 minute	.... **Back-up prompts** • Talk about the people/person. • Talk about the place. • Talk about other things in the photograph.
Interlocutor	Thank you. (Can I have the booklet please?) *Retrieve **Part 2** booklet.*

1B Having a party

Interlocutor	**B**, here is your photograph. It shows **some people having a party**. *Place **Part 2** booklet, open at **Task 1B**, in front of candidate.* **A**, you just listen. **B**, please tell us what you can see in the photograph.
Candidate B ⏲ approx. 1 minute	.... **Back-up prompts** • Talk about the people/person. • Talk about the place. • Talk about other things in the photograph.
Interlocutor	Thank you. (Can I have the booklet please?) *Retrieve **Part 2** booklet.*

1A

1B

Speaking Test 9 (Places to visit)

Parts 3 and 4 (6 minutes)

Part 3

Interlocutor: Now, in this part of the test you're going to talk about something together for about two minutes. I'm going to describe a situation to you.

Place Part 3 booklet, open at Task 1, in front of the candidates.

Some friends are choosing somewhere to go at the weekend. Here are some places they could go to.

Talk together about the different places, and say which would be most interesting.

All right? Now, talk together.

Candidates ……………………………………………..

⏱ *approx. 2–3 minutes*

Interlocutor: Thank you. (Can I have the booklet please?) *Retrieve Part 3 booklet.*

Part 4

Interlocutor: *Use the following questions, as appropriate:*

- **What places do you enjoy visiting the most? (Why?)**
- **Do you like to visit old places, like ancient sites? (Why?/Why not?)**
- **Do you prefer a quiet weekend or a weekend with lots of activities? (Why?)**
- **What different places can you get to easily from your town or city?**
- **Which do you think is more interesting: going to the countryside or going to a big city? (Why?)**

Select any of the following prompts, as appropriate:
- **How/what about you?**
- **Do you agree?**
- **What do you think?**

Thank you. **That is the end of the test.**

Places to visit

Cambridge B1 Preliminary

Speaking

Test 10

© 2025 Prosperity Education.
'Cambridge B1 Preliminary' and 'PET' are brands belonging to The Chancellor, Masters and Scholars of the University of Cambridge and are not associated with Prosperity Education or its products.

Speaking Test 10 Part 1 (2–3 minutes)

Phase 1

Interlocutor

To both candidates	Good morning / afternoon / evening.
	Can I have your mark sheets, please?
	Hand over the mark sheets to the Assessor.
	I'm .... and this is ....
To Candidate A	What's your name? How old are you?
	Thank you.
To Candidate B	And what's your name? How old are you?
	Thank you.

	Back-up prompts
B, what are your favourite school subjects?	What lessons do you enjoy at school?
	Do you like English?
How do you get to school?	Do you go by bus?
	How far is your school from your house?
	Is it a big school?
Thank you.	
And **A**, what are your favourite school subjects?	What lessons do you enjoy at school?
	Do you like English?
How do you get to school?	Do you go by bus?
	How far is your school from your house?
	Is it a big school?
Thank you.	

Phase 2

Interlocutor

Select one or more questions from the list to ask each candidate.

Ask Candidate A first.

	Back-up prompts
Tell us about a subject you like.	Which subject do you like? (Why?)
How often do you travel to another city?	Do you often go on a train? (Why?/Why not?) When did you last go to another city? (Why?)
What do you usually do after school?	Do you go to any after-school clubs? Do you go on social media in the evening?
What's your favourite food?	How often do you eat it?

Thank you.

Speaking B1 | Ten tests for the Cambridge Preliminary

Speaking Test 10 | **Part 2 (2–3 minutes)**

1A Helping on a farm

Interlocutor	Now I'd like each of you to talk on your own about something. I'm going to give each of you a photograph and I'd like you to talk about it. **A**, here is your photograph. It shows **a child helping on a farm**. *Place **Part 2** booklet, open at **Task 1A**, in front of candidate.* **B**, you just listen. **A**, please tell us what you can see in the photograph.
Candidate A ⏱ *approx. 1 minute*	....
	Back-up prompts • Talk about the people/person. • Talk about the place. • Talk about other things in the photograph.
Interlocutor	Thank you. (Can I have the booklet please?) *Retrieve **Part 2** booklet.*

1B Playing a game

Interlocutor	**B**, here is your photograph. It shows **some people playing a game**. *Place **Part 2** booklet, open at **Task 1B**, in front of candidate.* **A**, you just listen. **B**, please tell us what you can see in the photograph.
Candidate B ⏱ *approx. 1 minute*	....
	Back-up prompts • Talk about the people/person. • Talk about the place. • Talk about other things in the photograph.
Interlocutor	Thank you. (Can I have the booklet please?) *Retrieve **Part 2** booklet.*

Speaking Test 10 (Hobbies)

Parts 3 and 4 (6 minutes)

Part 3

Interlocutor   Now, in this part of the test you're going to talk about something together for about two minutes. I'm going to describe a situation to you.

Place Part 3 booklet, open at Task 1, in front of the candidates.

A girl is bored and wants to start a new hobby.

Here are some hobbies she could start.

Talk together about the different hobbies, and say which would be most interesting.

All right? Now, talk together.

Candidates ……………………………………………………………..

⏲ *approx. 2–3 minutes*

Interlocutor   Thank you. (Can I have the booklet please?) *Retrieve Part 3 booklet.*

Part 4

Interlocutor   *Use the following questions, as appropriate:*

- **What hobbies do you do? How long have you done each one for?**
- **Do you prefer hobbies you can do indoors, or outdoor hobbies? (Why?)**
- **Do you prefer hobbies which involve other people or ones you can do on your own? (Why?)**
- **Do you like hobbies that involve creating things or hobbies that involve being active? (Why?)**
- **Which new hobby do you think would be most interesting to start? (Why?)**

Select any of the following prompts, as appropriate:
- **How/what about you?**
- **Do you agree?**
- **What do you think?**

Thank you. **That is the end of the test.**

Hobbies

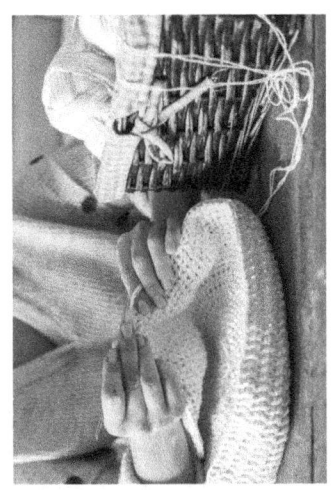
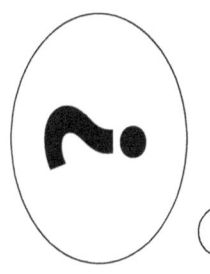

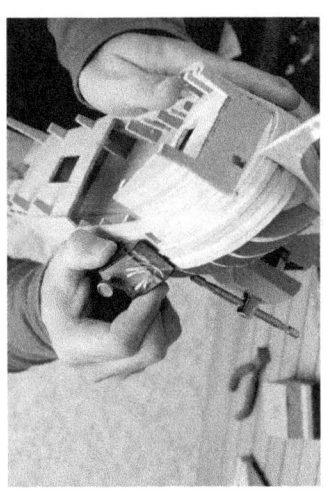

Bonus content

selected from:

Test 1 – Part 1	Cambridge B2 First: Speaking
2 minutes (3 minutes for groups of three)	

Candidates' background

Good morning/afternoon/evening. My name is ………….. and this is my colleague ………….. .

And your names are?

Can I have your mark sheets, please?

Thank you.

- Where are you from, *(Candidate A)*?
- And you, *(Candidate B)*?

First, we'd like to know something about you.

Select one or more questions from any of the following categories, as appropriate.

Sport

- When was the last time you played a sport? …… (What did you do?)
- Do you prefer individual sports or team sports? …… (Why?)
- How often do you watch live sport? …… (Would you like to watch more?) …… (Why? / Why not?)
- Is there a sports event you would really like to go to in the future? …… (Why? / Why not?)

Food

- Do you prefer eating at home or in restaurants? …… (Why?)
- Tell us about a special meal you can remember.
- Have you ever taken cooking classes? …… (Tell us about it. / Would you like to?)
- Is there a type of food you'd like to try? …… (Which one?) …… (Why?)

Films

- Do you prefer watching films at home or going to the cinema? …… (Why?)
- What type of films do you like the most? …… (Why?)
- Tell us about a famous film from (candidate's country).
- Have you ever wanted to act or make films? …… (Why? / Why not?)

Cambridge B2 First: Speaking	Test 1 – Part 2
	4 minutes (6 minutes for groups of three)

1 Ways of studying	2 Shopping for clothes

Interlocutor In this part of the test, I'm going to give each of you two photographs. I'd like you to talk about your photographs on your own for about a minute, and also to answer a question about your partner's photographs.

(Candidate A), it's your turn first. Here are your photographs. They show **people studying in different ways**.

*Place **Part 2** booklet, open at **Task 1**, in front of Candidate A.*

I'd like you to compare the photographs, and say **what you think the people are enjoying about studying in these ways**.

All right?

Candidate A

....

1 minute

Interlocutor Thank you.

(Candidate B), **do you often use the internet for your studies? …… (Why? / Why not?)**

Candidate B

....

Approximately 30 seconds

Interlocutor Thank you. (Can I have the booklet, please?) *Retrieve **Part 2** booklet.*

Now, *(Candidate B)*, here are your photographs. They show **people shopping for clothes in different ways**.

*Place **Part 2** booklet, open at **Task 2**, in front of Candidate B.*

I'd like you to compare the photographs, and say **why you think the people have chosen to shop for clothes in these ways**.

All right?

Candidate B

....

1 minute

Interlocutor Thank you.

(Candidate A), **do you prefer shopping for clothes with other people or alone? …… (Why?)**

Candidate A

....

Approximately 30 seconds

Interlocutor Thank you. (Can I have the booklet, please?) *Retrieve **Part 2** booklet.*

Test 1 – Part 2
Booklet 1

Cambridge B2 First: Speaking

What are the people enjoying about studying in these ways?

Cambridge B2 First: Speaking

Test 1 – Part 2
Booklet 2

Why have the people chosen to shop for clothes in these ways?

Test 1 – Part 3
4 minutes (5 minutes for groups of three)

Cambridge B2 First: Speaking

Attracting young professionals

Interlocutor Now, I'd like you to talk about something together for about two minutes *(3 minutes for groups of three)*.

I'd like you to imagine that a city is preparing an advertising campaign to attract more young professionals to live in the area. Here are some ideas they are thinking about and a question for you to discuss. First you have some time to look at the task.

*Place **Part 3** booklet, open at **Task 3**, in front of the candidates. Allow 15 seconds.*

Now, talk to each other about **why these factors would make young professionals want to live in the city.**

Candidate A

....

2 minutes (3 minutes for groups of three)

Interlocutor Thank you. Now you have about a minute to decide **which idea would be the best for the town.**

Candidate B

....

Approximately 30 seconds

Interlocutor Thank you. (Can I have the booklet, please?) *Retrieve **Part 3** booklet.*

Part 4
4 minutes (6 minutes for groups of three)

Interlocutor *Use the following questions, in order, as appropriate:*

| *Select any of the following prompts, as appropriate:* |
| • **What do you think?** |
| • **Do you agree?** |
| • **And you?** |

As well as young professionals, what other types of people might cities want to attract? ...... **(Why?)**

Some people say that it is unfair for cities to receive so much investment and that rural areas should be improved instead. Do you agree? ...... **(Why? / Why not?)**

What can companies do to help staff who have just moved to the area? ......

What are the most enjoyable things to do on a city break in (candidate's country)?

Some people say that remote working will transform cities. What do you think?

Would you agree that cities are designed for the needs of young people? ...... **(Why? / Why not?)**

Interlocutor Thank you. That is the end of the test.

Cambridge B2 First: Speaking

Test 1 – Part 3
Booklet

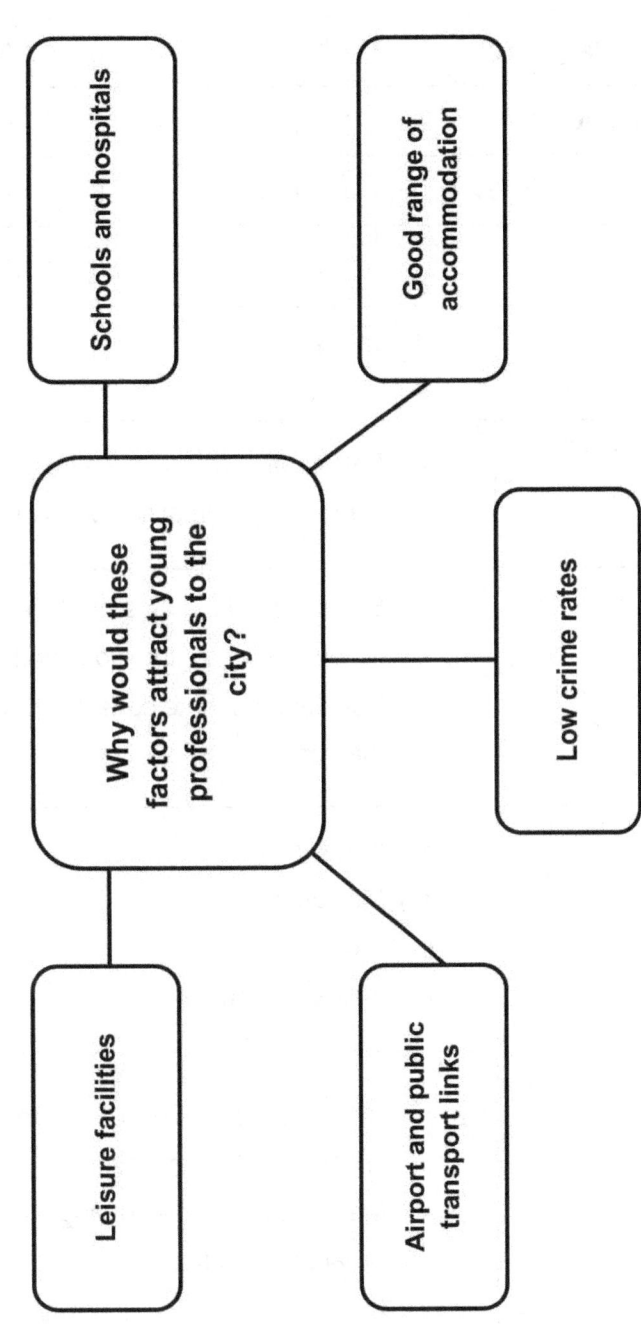

Speaking First — Mark sheet

Date | DD | MM | YY

Candidate _____

Marks available

Grammar and vocabulary	0	1	1.5	2	2.5	3	3.5	4	4.5	5
Discourse Management	0	1	1.5	2	2.5	3	3.5	4	4.5	5
Pronunciation	0	1	1.5	2	2.5	3	3.5	4	4.5	5
Interactive Communication	0	1	1.5	2	2.5	3	3.5	4	4.5	5

Item descriptors

Grammar and vocabulary *Control* *Range*	• Degree of control of grammatical forms. • Range of grammatical forms used.
Discourse Management *Extent* *Relevance* *Coherence* *Cohesion*	• Stretches of language produced. • Relevance of contributions and organisation of ideas. • Use of appropriate cohesive devices and discourse markers.
Pronunciation *Intonation* *Stress* *Individual sounds*	• Intelligibility • Intonation • Word stress • Individual sounds
Interactive Communication *Initiating* *Responding* *Development*	• Initiating, responding and linking contributions to other speakers' interventions. • Maintaining and developing interaction, and negotiating towards an outcome.

Cambridge B2 First

Speaking

Test 1 model answers

© 2025 Prosperity Education.
'Cambridge B2 First' and 'FCE' are brands belonging to The Chancellor, Masters and Scholars of the University of Cambridge and are not associated with Prosperity Education or its products.

Speaking First

Model answers – Test 1

The B2 First is usually taken by candidates who want to obtain a B2-level certificate, which corresponds to an upper-intermediate level of English.

As described by the Common European Framework of Reference for Languages (CEFRL), candidates with a B2 level are considered *independent vantage users*, thus being able to:

- understand the main ideas of complex tests
- interact with a certain degree of fluency and spontaneity both in written and oral form
- produce clear and detailed texts on a range of subjects.

The purpose of the following model answers is to provide teachers and candidates with an example of language production and test performance that would score a high mark in a real B2 First Speaking test.

Without being particularly complex, these answers contain grammatical and lexical features as well as a range of discourse resources suited to an upper-intermediate level of English (B2).

Please note that complete linguistic accuracy is not expected at B2 level, but only candidates whose performance is generally accurate will receive a high mark.

On pages 95–100, there are comments highlighting different aspects of the model answers, such as:

- the strategies candidates make use of to address some of the parts
- the ways in which candidates express their opinions
- how candidates interact with one another, etc.

The aim of these comments is to draw the reader's attention to important details that might help to achieve a successful performance in this part of the B2 First examination.

While reading the model answers and the examiner's comments, please bear in mind the following:

- The test is taken in pairs, and candidates are expected to interact with each other.
- The approximate timing of each part of the test is as follows:
    - Part 1: 2 minutes (pair) / 3 minutes (trio)
    - Part 2: 4 minutes (pair) / 6 minutes (trio)
    - Part 3: 4 minutes (pair) / 5 minutes (trio)
    - Part 4: 4 minutes (pair) / 6 minutes (trio)

These model answers would achieve a high score in a B2 First Speaking test, and so should be regarded as strong-performance answers that provide examples of the types of linguistic structures candidates are expected to produce at this level rather than examples of minimum performance to pass.

Model answers

Test 1 – Part 1 – Model answers

Interlocutor	Where are you from, Candidate A?
Candidate A	*I'm from Costa Rica, and I live in a town called Nicoya.*
Interlocutor	And you, Candidate B?
Candidate B	*I'm from Stockholm in Sweden, but I live in Rome.*
Interlocutor	Are you working or studying at the moment?
Candidate B	*I work for a logistics company as a customer services manager. I've been doing that for about five years.*
Interlocutor	And you?
Candidate A	*Well, I'm working as a sales assistant in a shop, you know, as a temporary job over the summer. But I'm planning to start a college course soon. I want to study computer science.*

Sport

- **When was the last time you played a sport?** *It was probably about a month ago, when I played football with some friends.*
- **Do you prefer individual sport or team sports?** *Well, I'm really into running and I like doing that on my own because I can listen to music.*
- **How often do you watch live sport?** *Well, I watch a lot of football on TV and they show a lot of important matches live. In terms of going to watch matches in person, I tend to watch my local team probably about once a month. It's really good fun even though we usually lose.*
- **Is there a sports event you would really like to go to in the future?** *If I had the chance to go and see some Olympic events, I'm sure it would be an amazing experience to get to see the most famous athletes in the world. But I don't think it's likely because it's so hard to get tickets for those kinds of events.*

Food

- **Do you prefer eating at home or in restaurants?** *I like both, to be honest. Now and then, it's fun to go to a restaurant, especially if you can try some new dishes and enjoy the atmosphere. But deep down, I guess it's more relaxing to have a home-cooked meal with friends.*
- **Tell us about a special meal you can remember.** *Probably when I was invited to the home of an Indian colleague and her family cooked me some incredible traditional dishes. I'd been to Indian restaurants before so I thought I knew what to expect but this was completely different. It was real, authentic Indian food.*
- **Have you ever taken cooking classes?** *Only in school, where the teacher would show us the basics of food preparation. In general, the recipes we got to try were pretty easy. I'd love to learn more about French food, though.*
- **Is there a type of food you'd like to try?** *Well, I'm curious about Vietnamese food. I'm a big fan of Asian cuisine, in other words, anything spicy or with noodles or rice, and as far as know, Vietnamese food is similar. I've also heard that it's quite diverse and healthy too.*

Speaking First

Films

- **Do you prefer watching films at home or going to the cinema?** *Definitely watching films at home. Going to the cinema just costs too much, because you've got to think about transport, tickets, not to mention the snacks as well. I don't see the point when you can just stream one instead.*
- **What type of films do you like the most?** *To be honest, I'm not a huge film fan. I suppose I'd say action films like Mission Impossible because you can just switch your brain off for a while because you don't have to worry about a complicated plot, or whatever. That's the main thing.*
- **Do you have a favourite film from Sweden?** *Well, pretty much everyone has heard of Ingmar Berman's films, I'd imagine. He's a very famous director, and I'd definitely recommend The Seventh Seal. I won't go into the plot because it's quite complex, but some of the scenes are iconic, especially the chess one, so it's worth watching for that reason.*
- **Have you ever wanted to act or make films?** *Well, I used to perform in school plays when I was younger but not anything serious. The idea of making films kind of appeals, though. My friends and I create short videos and upload them to social media. I enjoy the creative aspect of the editing and music, all that stuff.*

Test 1 – Part 2 – Model answers

Being active

Task 1 – Long turn

Interlocutor In this part of the test, I'm going to give each of you two photographs. I'd like you to talk about your photographs on your own for about a minute, and also to answer a question about your partner's photographs. *(Candidate A)* It's your turn first. Here are your photographs (photo A – three young people looking at a laptop and taking notes, photo B – children listening to a teacher in a classroom). They show people studying in different ways. I'd like you to compare the photographs, and say what you think the people in these photos are enjoying about studying in these ways. All right?

Candidate A OK, well, in the first picture there are three students who appear to be in a computer lab or somewhere like that. They may be working on a project together because the student with glasses looks like he's going to take notes. By contrast, the second picture is what I'd call a traditional classroom, with pupils sitting at separate desks, and the teacher explaining the information. One of the students has raised his hand so he might have misunderstood something.

Obviously, these photos illustrate two rather different approaches to studying or education. The students in the first picture are finding information for themselves, whereas in the classroom, the students' role is more passive. What I mean is that they're simply listening. Also, the students in the classroom look younger, so they're probably at school, whereas I'd guess the others are college or university students. Turning to what they might be enjoying about studying, well, the college students look very engaged, probably because they're giving their input and making decisions for themselves. With the second photo, the students can receive instant help by asking questions, and that can be motivating. I think this shows us the importance of getting feedback or support.

Interlocutor Thank you. (Candidate B), do you often use the internet for your studies?

Candidate B	*Well, in terms of language learning, I do, yes. You can find all sorts of useful videos to practise listening and I try to read online articles on a daily basis. And of course, the vast majority of information on social media is in English too, so that's another useful way to improve your skills.*
Interlocutor	Thank you. (*Can I have the booklet, please?*) Now, (*Candidate B*), here are your photographs. They show people shopping for clothes in different ways (photo A – a man using a computer to look at a clothing website, photo B – two women in a clothes shop, about to try on items). I'd like you to compare **two** of the photographs, and say why you think the people have chosen to shop for clothes in these ways. All right?
Candidate B	*Yes, OK, let's see. I'll start with the photo of the man. He seems to be at home, using a laptop to do some online shopping. It looks as if it's the website of a footwear company. He appears to be looking at men's shoes, so he might be choosing shoes for himself. In the photo, the man seems to be ready to pay for the item so he has probably made his decision. And of course, it's much more convenient to do that online instead of going around all the shops in person.*
	As for the second picture, I'd guess that those shoppers are more likely to make a purchase. We can see two young women in a fitting room of a shop. In particular, the one on the right has selected various items of clothing which she's about to try on. There's more of a sense of excitement about shopping in this photo, so I get the impression that they wanted to have a fun day out together rather than the convenience of online shopping.
Interlocutor	Thank you. (*Candidate A*), do you prefer shopping for clothes with other people or alone?
Candidate A	*Well, it depends. Things like t-shirts, well, I already have an idea of how they're going to fit and what suits me so it's pretty easy just to shop by myself. But if I do need a second opinion, I prefer going with my sister or a friend. Actually, my sister helped me pick an outfit for our cousin's wedding.*
Interlocutor	Thank you. (*Can I have the booklet, please?*)

Test 1 – Part 3 – Model answers

Attracting young professionals

Collaborative task

Interlocutor	Now, I'd like you to talk about something together for about **two** minutes. I'd like you to imagine that a city is preparing an advertising campaign to attract more young professionals to live in the area. Here are some ideas they are thinking about and a question for you to discuss. First you have some time to look at the task. Now, talk to each other about why these factors would make young professionals want to live in the city.
Candidate A	*Well then, would you like to start?*
Candidate B	*Sure, let's see. Well, obviously if you were thinking of moving to a new area, you'd want to know whether it's safe, so you'd probably research the crime rates, wouldn't you? But if we're talking specifically about young professionals, they'd probably have accommodation at the top of their list. What do you think?*
Candidate A	*Yes, that's right. I don't know about you, but I sort of imagine people at the start of their careers, so a city with a range of affordable places to rent would be ideal. And if they can find attractive accommodation near where they work, it'll presumably save them time in terms of*

Speaking First

	commuting. But I suppose that brings us to transport. Do you think that would be an important consideration?
Candidate B	Oh, most definitely, it's one they should think about if they've got family in other parts of the country. And they might be asked to travel a lot for work as well. They're more important than cinemas or restaurants, for example, although you might disagree.
Candidate A	Well, I see your point and I do think transport is vital, but you seem to put it ahead of leisure facilities. For me, they're probably of equal importance because moving to a new city is a major decision, isn't it? Would you really be willing to move somewhere if there was nothing to do, or no ways of making new friends?
Candidate B	That's true. So if we look at it as a permanent move, then you might also look at other things too, like schools and hospitals. You'd want to settle somewhere that has facilities for children, for example.
Candidate A	Yes, I hadn't thought about that but it makes sense. In fact, I'd argue they're all important..
Interlocutor	Thank you. Now you have about a minute to decide which idea would be the best for the town.
Candidate B	Perhaps you'd like to start this time?
Candidate A	Of course, it seems that we both feel that young professionals are likely to pay particular attention to transport and accommodation, don't we? If so, the city should probably focus on those in their advertising campaigns. Do you agree?
Candidate B	Well, I suppose so. I mean, obviously the city should highlight all the other factors too, especially if they are strengths.
Candidate A	Mmm.. so are you saying that the city should analyse what it does best and build their advertising around that? I'm not sure about that. It would be better to put transport and accommodation at the centre of the advertising. Accommodation will definitely attract young professionals because it's so hard to find places to live.
Candidate B	Don't get me wrong, we're on the same page. The city should focus on accommodation to attract young professionals, and maybe this could be linked to information about efficient transport connections too. But as well as that, it should mention other aspects so as to boost their chances of success.
Candidate A	Great, so I think we're in agreement then.

Test 1 – Part 4 – Model answers

Question-based discussion

Interlocutor	As well as young professionals, what other types of people might cities want to attract?
Candidate A	Well, honestly, there needs to be as much diversity as possible. What I mean is that cities rely on all sorts of residents, including families, students, retired people or whatever. You see, they all have a role to play in society because they have different skills and experiences, don't they? I'd argue that this mix of perspectives builds strong communities.
Interlocutor	Some people believe that it is unfair for cities to receive so much investment and that rural areas should be improved instead. Do you agree?
Candidate B	Well, as we've been discussing, I don't see it that way at all. The truth is that investing in cities makes the most sense because it'll have the biggest impact on more people. For example,

	there are so many people commuting to cities each day for work, so it makes sense that the public transport links are upgraded there first. But it's still important to invest in rural areas too.
Interlocutor	*(Candidate A)*, what do you think?
Candidate A	*I'm not sure really. I guess these sorts of decisions have to be taken after weighing up many important factors. In my country, for instance, a lot of investment has gone into improving living standards in rural areas, and to a certain extent it has sort of encouraged more young people to settle in those places instead of migrating to cities.*
Interlocutor	What can companies do to help staff who have just moved to the area?
Candidate A	*That's a difficult question. If you mean the things that we've already been talking about, they could offer free transport passes or help employees find somewhere to live. And I've heard that some companies even provide accommodation for staff, which would be very useful.*
Interlocutor	*(Candidate B)*, do you agree?
Candidate B	*Well, they're definitely good suggestions but I'd like to add something. What about organising social activities? It doesn't have to be anything fancy, but maybe a night out at a restaurant with colleagues? It would help break the ice which in turn would make the new employees feel more settled.*
Interlocutor	What are the most enjoyable things to do on a city break in Nicoya?
Candidate A	*Well, if you're talking about a couple of days, I'd personally say walking up La Cruz hill is a must because you'll get an amazing panoramic view of the whole town. To make the most of it, you should aim to go there at sunset. Oh, and I'd recommend checking out the farmers' market where you can try so many delicious local specialities. You won't regret it, trust me!*
Interlocutor	Some people say that remote working will transform cities. What do you think?
Candidate B	*Do you mean in terms of what people use cities for? As far as the numbers of people in city centres are concerned, the impact can already be seen because some city centres are far quieter than they once were. On the face of it, that sounds like a positive. After all, less traffic congestion will eventually benefit the environment. But what about local businesses? I say this with a heavy heart because many of the places where I loved killing time with friends are closing down. So given all that, I'd basically say it's true, but I hope they don't turn into ghost towns.*
Interlocutor	Would you agree that cities are designed for the needs of young people?
Candidate A	*I don't know if I can answer objectively, but I suppose they are, to be honest. Cities are vibrant, fast-paced places that are always changing, and I associate that more with young people. On top of that, most cities have entertainment venues, universities and places like that right in the heart of things. It makes sense, because young people are the ones who tend to drive less so they need to have easy access to those sorts of amenities.*
Interlocutor	Thank you. That is the end of the test.

www.ingramcontent.com/pod-product-compliance
Lightning Source LLC
Chambersburg PA
CBHW081103070526
44584CB00021B/3183